HALLOWEEN
COLORING BOOK FOR ADULTS

Relaxing Designs

Pumpkins, Ghosts. Skulls, Mandalas, Bats and More
25 Black Background Illustrations

Time to relax, color, express your creativity and have a spooky and fun Halloween!

Copyright © 2020 by Jocky Books

All rights reserved. No part of this book may be reproduced or used in any manner without written permission of the copyright owner except for the use of quotations in a book review.

First paperback edition October 2020

THIS SPOOKY BOOK BELONGS TO

Color Test

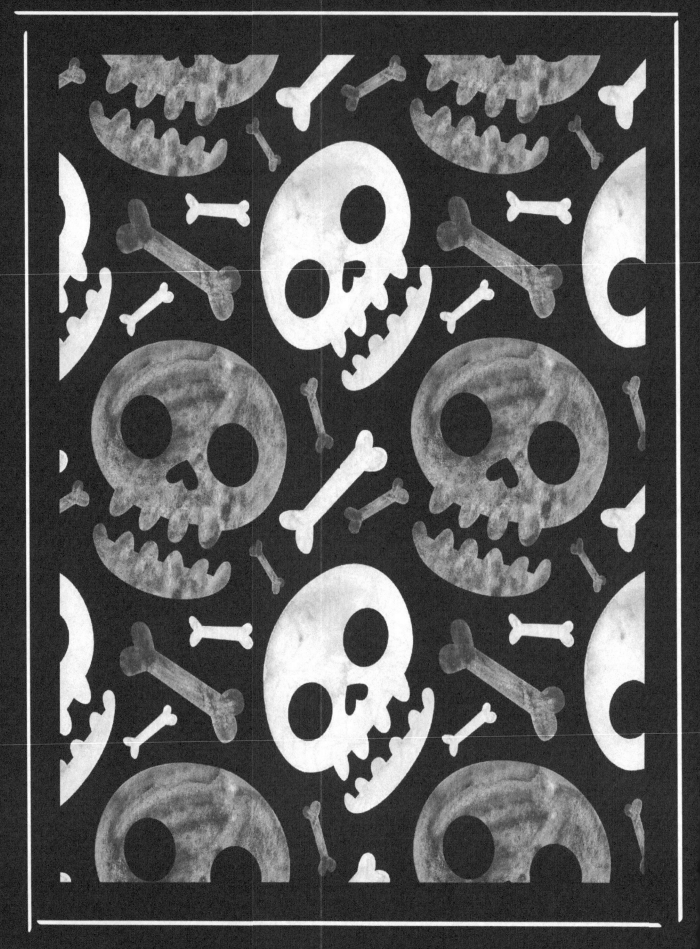

HAPPY HALLOWEEN

Simply Boo-tiful!

Hello Halloween

We would love to hear from you.
Please, consider leaving a review with your opinion and recommendations.
Thanks a lot for your support!

Made in the USA
Columbia, SC
09 December 2024

48895556R00059